For

Now ??
to England (Cambridge)
to find dog books!
Happy Birthday,
Love, Cynth

THE
DOG DAY
BOOK

Cameradog, 1998

THE
DOG DAY
BOOK

PHOTOGRAPHS BY
John Drysdale

TEXT BY
Margaret Regan

To Nello and Puccini,
playfellows and friends

The photographs in this book have not been
electronically altered or manipulated.

First published in the US (as MY LOVE UNLEASHED) in 2002 by
St Martin's Press, 175 Fifth Avenue,
New York, NY 10010

This edition published in Great Britain in 2002 by
Michael O'Mara Books Limited
9 Lion Yard, Tremadoc Road,
London SW4 7NQ

ISBN 1-84317-004-3

3 5 7 9 10 8 6 4 2

Book design by James Sinclair

Edited by Brad Wood

Printed and bound by Eurolitho SpA, Milan

INTRODUCTION

The dog is man's best and oldest friend. Throughout history dogs have displayed extraordinary loyalty to their owners. Mary Queen of Scots' lapdog defended her mistress's body after she had been beheaded. Greyfriars Bobby waited by his master's grave for years until death reunited them. Most people would agree that a dog's love for its owner is the most unconditional and unquestioning of them all. In the 1800s, Lord Byron praised his beloved dog for possessing 'all the virtues of man, without his vices.' And Mark Twain later proclaimed, 'Heaven goes by favour. If it went by merit, you would stay out and your dog would go in.'

Later still, first on the continent of Africa and then throughout Europe, the dog delighted and seduced the merry photographic eye of John Drysdale. This African-born British photographer has been studying and photographing dogs for decades – celebrating their rich personalities, venerating their intelligence and large-heartedness. His patience and playfulness, his endless capacity for joy and affection and humour, seem to mirror the characteristics of the extraordinary dogs in the photographs. Luckily for us, seventy of

Drysdale's remarkable dog portraits are published together here in this delightful album.

Throughout this book, and often in the same picture, tenderness and (dog) dignity rub shoulders with the comic and the quirky. And with the wondrous: the variety of interspecies friendships pictured here reminds us that dogs have a special genius for togetherness. Enchanted and enchanting, marvelling in the moment, these dogs are friends to the world. They have been caught by Drysdale's cat-like camera while living in full view of the world – openly and busily and inquisitively, with an astonishing gift for adaptability, and with a manner uncritical and unfeigned. Each picture evokes the deep, abiding mysteries of dogdom and the enduring pleasures of mankind's oldest and most constant companion. And in each unique Drysdale dog we can see all dogs as they share an unconditional kinship with the world, a secret understanding that inspires love and lasts forever.

Friend of the Danes, 1970

"Dogs are not our whole life, but they make our lives whole."
—Roger Caras, *Dog People*

"I don't say we ought to misbehave, but we should look as though we could."
—Oscar Wilde

Caught at the Kitchen Door, 1998

Dinner Hour, 1998

The little dourcouli monkey, orphaned and traumatized, was paired with the Chihuahua pup for company and comfort.

Dog Sips Milk, 1968

Fresh Egg, 1970

Here is proud Flash the Labrador, who learned to collect the eggs laid by his owner's hens—and never cracked a single one. He did this daily and diligently and was always rewarded with a biscuit at teatime.

Dainty Dining, 1996

Puplets Snooze in Dollhouse Bed, 1993

Shoe Fetish, 1996

The chimp loves the puppy and the puppy loves the chimp. But the puppy also loves shoes—loves to drag them about, climb inside them, and chew them beyond repair.

Aztec Flying, 1970

Aztec the cocker spaniel had a peculiar habit of raising her head rapidly and abruptly, causing her long, beautiful ears to fly.

Suzie the bulldog's puppies had recently been sold when someone brought three tiny gray squirrels to the farm where she lived, near Southam, England. Assuming they had been abandoned by their mother, the farmer undertook the laborious task of feeding the frail little squirrels with a syringe every two hours. He then successfully transferred nursing to Suzie, whose strong maternal instincts welcomed and protected them. As the squirrels recovered and began growing normally, they accepted the bulldog as their mother and seemed domesticated by her. Meanwhile, Suzie of the fearsome look and gentle nature was happy in her mothering role, and she was revivified—no longer forlorn over the loss of her puppies.

Bulldog Watch, 1969

Market Day, 1996

Out for a Walk, 1994

The basset hound enjoyed being a "supervisor," forever following his mistress while she tended a large number of horses. But when she invited him to join the working class one day, he eagerly accepted. Thereafter, whenever she led a horse, the dependable dog would follow, leading another.

The Shetland Sheepdog and the Philippines Cockatoo, 1994

The sheepdog and the cockatoo are best friends and play at "mock battles" every day. They are inseparable—except when the cockatoo goes off on her daily free-flying exercise. When she returns to their South London home, she taps on the window for entrance.

In London, certain streets were once designated "play streets" and were closed to traffic. Though the goalposts in this play street were imaginary, the dog and a small group of boys were engrossed in a rousing football game, with the dog being treated as an equal player and acting as goalkeeper. He was such a skilled goalie that none of the boys was able to score.

Dog Goalie, 1955

Tennis, Anyone?, 1967

Having a cavernous mouth, and thereby having developed the knack of fielding two balls, the Great Dane became an ideal "ball boy" during her owner's tennis matches.

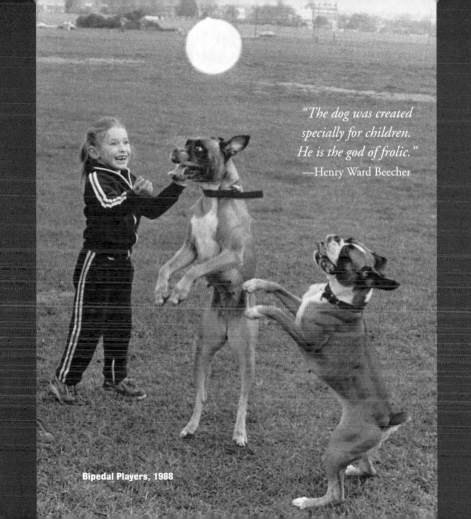

"The dog was created specially for children. He is the god of frolic."
—Henry Ward Beecher

Bipedal Players, 1988

Bikers, 1989

Joy Ride, 1990

Rover the Taxi Dog, 1967

After long walks together, Rover the Labrador and his owner always returned home by taxi. Rover then began taking long walks on his own, after which he would show up at the taxi rank for the ride home. He was able to recognize London cabs and distinguish them from ordinary automobiles. If the taxi drivers happened to be busy speaking with customers, he would bark until they noticed that he, too, was queuing for a cab. The drivers used to check the address and telephone number on his collar and ring up the owner, who always asked them to drive Rover home. Eventually, all the taxi men knew the dog and one of them would automatically give him a ride home. Eventually, too, Rover's regal rides became quite expensive for his (uncomplaining) owner.

Formal Introduction, 1981

Mama Tigress, 1989

The puppy loves this Bengal tigress who, having been bottle-fed as a cub, is very tame and mothers the dog. She had to be taken away from her own mother, who had a history of killing her cubs. But she's obviously grown up without her mother's murderous habits—otherwise, the little dog would be inside her.

Ear Nibble, 1967

The orphaned llama and the Rhodesian Ridgeback became fast friends and played and stayed together day and night.

Labrador-Golden Retriever and Baby Cotton-Eared Marmoset, 1998

The rare baby marmoset, one of triplets, was reared via a medicine dropper because his mother could supply milk for two only. In the risky early weeks, when all marmosets must cling to their mothers, this kind and gentle dog assumed the mama role.

Chez Moi, 1996

"Our perfect companions never have fewer than four feet."
—Colette

Portrait of a Lion Dog, 1996

"… a rag of wolf's tongue redpanting from his jaws."
—James Joyce, *Ulysses*

Canine Coiffure, 1969

"The greatest pleasure of a dog is that you may make a fool of yourself with him and not only will he not scold you, but he will make a fool of himself too."
—Samuel Butler

The owner of a London hair salon always brought Rex, his Labrador-mastiff, to work—and Rex always sat on any chair not occupied. The regular customers thought it perfectly normal, routine, to find Rex seated beside them. But people new to the salon were always asking why a dog was sitting under the dryer. And so the owner made a curler wig for Rex. When anyone was particularly pesky on a busy day, persistently questioning the seating preferences of Rex, the owner would whip out the wig, pop it on the dog's head, and he and Rex would look at the customer as if to say, Why do you *think* he's sitting there? Obviously to prove that he can look as foolish as humans!

Boston Terrier Laugh, 1992

The shy and gentle Boston terrier, inappropriately named Bossy, was constantly being harassed by rough, neighboring dogs near his home in Oundle, England. When his mistress was asked to bottle-feed an abandoned lion cub, she brought it to Bossy for company. They became friends, and as Sylvia the lion cub grew bigger, she became very protective of the Boston terrier. The aggressive dogs wisely avoided the pair, and Bossy, at last free of their torment and happy with his beloved Sylvia, smiled and laughed a lot.

Watch Dog, 1985

On an average day, this cairn cross terrier spends half his time on the roof, which he reaches by jumping from a bank to a shed to another sloping roof —thence to the lofty heights where he presumably enjoys the peace and the view. Outside the pub are signs saying PLEASE DO NOT REPORT DOG ON ROOF—HE LIVES THERE.

These two are inseparable friends, even though the Himalayan golden eagle once killed a wolf in Pakistan.

Dog and Eagle in the Welsh Mountains, 1967

Dog and Owl, 1968

Unclaimed by its mother after falling out of the nest, the owl grew up with this crossbred Pekingese-griffon and adopted the dog's habits—staying awake most of the day and sleeping at night. The owl even tried to imitate the dog's bark, with limited success.

Bird Dog, 1988

A wild mute swan strayed from her territory on the River Thames, in England, and was badly injured and blinded in an attack by other swans. For a wild bird this meant certain death from predators. She was rescued, however, and after treatment at an animal hospital she was fed by a tube and recovered all but her sight. The swan soon accepted the company—and eventual friendship—of a German shepherd, whom she would follow by scent, using the dog as her eyes. Wearing a specially made harness attached to a long cord, the swan was brought to the river each day for exercise and a swim. She would then be returned to her friend and protector and guide, the German shepherd, on whose back she would happily nestle.

Swan Nestling on German Shepherd, 1994

"*I am his Highness' dog at Kew;*
Pray tell me, sir, whose dog are you?"

—Alexander Pope, engraved on
the collar of a dog he gave to His
Royal Highness in 1738

Big Dog, Little Dog, 1992

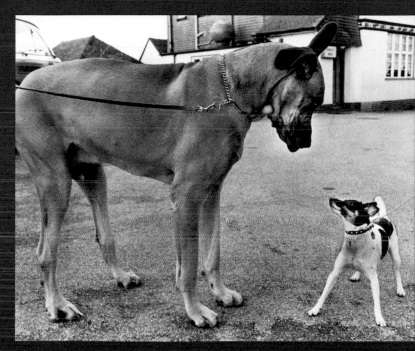

First Encounter, 1086

Puppy-Loving Chimp, 1970

The Kiss, 1994

Adoring Love, 1997

Adoring Love, 1980

"…the Love that moves the sun and the other stars."
—Dante Alighieri, *Paradiso*

Comfort of Friends, 1994

Though raised as a household pet, the basset hound gave up the comforts of life in his owners' home for the spartan environment of the stables, where he had formed a strange and lasting bond with a young camel.

Wolf Cubs and Kid, 1994

The Rescued and the Proud, 1970

While walking along the beach, the mastiff-Golden Labrador found this seagull with a missing wing and gently carried it home to his owners. He then promptly adopted the little gull. Strangely, so did the three cats with whom he lived. Via the infliction of an occasional sharp peck, the one-winged seagull quickly took over and became boss of the house—but with affection unchanging for his dear dog friend and rescuer.

Fisher Folk, 1985

Noble Profile, 1994

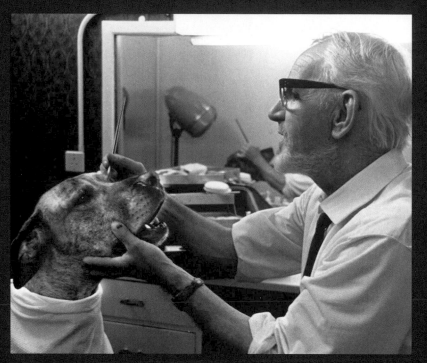

The Film Star, 1968

The Great Dane was a professional actor, starring in a film in production at Pinewood Studios near London, where the James Bond movies were made. This canine star shared the same makeup facilities as the human stars.

The Survivor, 1996

Very rare and very old, Lowchen lion dogs flourished from the fourteenth through the seventeenth centuries and were portrayed in many Rembrandt paintings. They were thought to be extinct at the end of World War II. But the last few Lowchens in existence—about six—were found in 1945 in Brussels, where the indomitable Madame Bennert had hidden them during the war.

Top Dog, 1969

This pup, a Basenji (a barkless hunting dog from the Congo) crossed with an Alsatian, enjoys riding on a giant Seychelles tortoise.

Puma Cub Exploring English Pointer, 1991

Getting the Phone, 1998

This helpful Lhasa apso once won the title of Britain's Most Intelligent Dog.

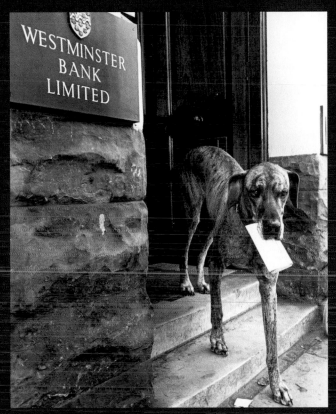

Getting the Money, 1968

The Lookout, 1975

Bunny Bower, 1985

Follow the Leader, 1975

A bulldog and a five-year-old girl could not resist exploring a hollow log, which the girl's grandfather had just delivered so it could be chopped up for firewood.

Follow the Fun, 1983

Recognition, 1969

Two crested species face-to-face. The Chinese crested dog and the Moran crested cockerel live on the same farm.

Recognition, 1991

In Harness, 1970

Resembling a junior Santa Claus with his rein-dogs, the baby was actually a convenient hitching post for the five Harlequin Great Danes, who had just returned from a walk and were patiently waiting while their mistress closed the gates.

Rolls-Royce and Chauffeur, 1968

"The best thing about a man is his dog." —Proverb

Evening Walk, 1999

This crossbred bullterrier enjoyed long walks with his owner until arthritis developed in his rear joints. The man then built a cart from sections of a baby stroller, harnessed his dog, and their happy walks together resumed.

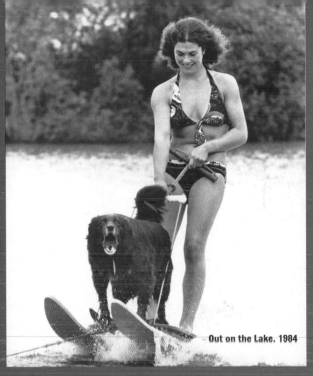

Out on the Lake, 1984

In Rutland, England, the Labrador-collie was not content to wait on the shore and watch her mistress waterskiing. After each ski run, she would swim out into the lake and retrieve her owner's skis, often struggling to get on them herself. Eventually, her mistress tried an experiment: She clamped a board onto the skis to see if they could ski together and if the dog would like it. The dog loved it, every minute of it, and she would bark happily, triumphantly, and continually throughout her water-ski rides.

Terry the Tree Dog, 1988

In puppyhood, Terry the Jack Russell terrier retrieved sticks thrown by his Devonshire owner. When the stick once accidentally landed in a conifer tree, his master was amazed to see him climbing the tree after it. Terry then made a daily habit of tree-climbing and would appear after a few seconds in the top branches, often as high as twenty to thirty feet. He would sometimes stay high in the tree through rain, snow, gales, even lightning, and seemed to enjoy the reactions of people gesticulating and calling to him from the ground. He seemed to have a sense of humor.

A Polite Yawn, 1993

A Big Yawn, 1998

Giant Yawn, 1970

Loving Look, 1970

"As he lay on the sofa at Miss Barrett's feet,
glory and delight coursed through his veins."
—Virginia Woolf, *Flush: A Biography*
(of Elizabeth Barrett Browning's cocker spaniel, Flush)

John Drysdale

Born in Uganda and raised in remote regions then teeming with wildlife, British photographer John Drysdale took his first pictures in Africa, using a two-thousand-gallon water tank as his (very hot) darkroom. His father, Kenneth Drysdale, had been one of the first to organize and conduct wild animal safaris, in Uganda and Kenya, beginning in 1927. Though he eventually arranged safaris for nearly all the crowned heads of Europe and a succession of Americans—from the Duke of Windsor to the Vanderbilts—a major part of Kenneth Drysdale's work was guiding and advising British and Hollywood filmmakers shooting on location in Africa. The presence and importance of animals and cameras, then, was a regular part of John Drysdale's early life.

Visiting relatives in Surrey, England, Drysdale received an invitation to study at the Guildford College of Art, noted for its program in photography. His studies completed, he remained in England and worked for many years in London, with Norman Parkinson at Vogue Studios and with Cecil Beaton as court photographer for the Royal Family. His first major assignment was assisting Beaton in photographing all the royals of Europe, in Buckingham Palace, after the coronation ceremony of Queen Elizabeth II in 1953. Prince Charles and Princess Anne, then small children in high spirits, were running about and had to be repeatedly carried back into the portrait groups—a nightmare, since the royals were roasting under hot lights and needed to "freeze" for pictures, most of which were ruined by excessive movement.

In the meantime, Drysdale began photographing unposed children without royal titles, in the streets of London, and his first successes in Fleet Street were for picture stories of these city scenes. His diverse daily work—including fashion and advertising, portraits of royalty and celebrities, architectural interiors and gardens, and photojournalism—never hindered his studies of children nor lessened his abiding interest in animals, both wild and domestic. He returned to Africa several times to photograph animals in various wildlife areas. In 1992, he visited the primeval wilderness of the Okavango Delta, one of the last truly wild places on earth.

John Drysdale's publishing credits and exhibitions are extensive, and his renown is worldwide, especially for his photographs of unusual interspecies bonding and of children. His awards include prizes from British Press Pictures of the Year and from World Press Photo. He lives in England.